THOUGI̶ ̶ ̶T̶E̶R̶S̶
FOR LONELY TIMES

Contents

Foreword

Loneliness, the theme of this small book, is something many of us, one day, may come to know.

It comes about sometimes simply because we live too long. A few of us outlive all our loved ones, and even our closest friends. We are left behind to live alone, to worry alone, to be ill alone, even to die alone. In the darkest of our moments we even come to regret we were made so strong.

For others loneliness seems to have been almost inborn. It takes the form of a cruel shyness, and a lack of confidence. Such people find it easier to withdraw than to mix. They can go to a University and yet never be fully part of it, hold down a good job, yet never be at ease with the people they serve. They find their loneliness at its most distressing when they are surrounded by people.

Loneliness comes with some professions. Those who have authority fear to trust lest they be exploited. Those who amass wealth fear the spurious affection that riches may bring. Actors can be lonely people and only be themselves on a stage. Clergy can experience a real loneliness as they come to grips with the world around them that understands little and cares less for the Faith to which they have dedicated their lives. There can be an isolation that is loneliness indeed for the dangerously ill and frightened.

No one has to be ashamed of being alone in life. That's no one's fault. More often than not, it is simply the way circumstances have been shaped. It only becomes hurtful and damaging, when loneliness takes over and sets about destroying the quality of what should be seen as a God-given life.

In the pages of this book you will find described many shared situations and many known heartaches. Yours may well be among them. They have been highlighted and illustrated by a kindly eye and a loving pen. What he does is not mere diagnosis. The writer has understanding and help to offer and longs to give them wherever he can.

The strange fact is that it has come from the pen of a man who is the least lonely I have ever known. He is an extrovert in every sense of the word, bubbling over with energy both physical and mental. He teaches Judo and Drama; he goes in for weightlifting. He belongs to many Fellowships and, long before he became a Priest, was an active member of his Church. No one could ever accuse him of being shy with words. Above all, he has a loving family background and an almost inexhaustible circle of friends. He can have been alone seldom and, as far as we can ever judge from outside, lonely never.

But that in no way inhibits him from creating this book. All those who have a worthwhile Faith long to share it with others. Those who have come to an inner peace cannot bear to see others around them struggling through tensions and anxiety. Here a very unlonely man, who has found much joy and love in the world around him, seeks to share what he has found with others who will have needs and problems other than his own. If the lonely find companionship and direction and hope from anything he has written, it will be a rich reward for him - and he will ascribe it all, not to any gifts of his, but to the kindly hand of a loving God.

Canon Stanley Mogford
Cardiff

Introduction

The problem of Loneliness

Loneliness is the dark side of independence: the price each man and woman pays for being an individual. To be a living, thinking being, aware of his or her own existence, makes each one of us vulnerable to loneliness.

We may try all through our lives to raise defences and build barriers against it, but there are times when all human defences collapse and all man-made barriers are broken down — and then the black tide of loneliness floods in.

Because it is an invisible enemy, we are not aware that at some time or another we all succumb to it; one of its worst weapons against us is the feeling we have that we are bearing it alone. Everyone else seems to be more popular, to have more friends and more hobbies, distractions and interests than we do — in the profoundest depth of loneliness we believe that we are suffering it entirely by ourselves. That, of course, makes it so much worse.

The first rung on the ladder that leads us out of the abysmal pit of loneliness is the knowledge that at least we are not alone in enduring it: we have not been singled our for this particular misfortune — being lonely is an innate risk that all human beings must run simply because we are human.

The busiest wife, mother, surgeon, priest, business executive or fireman can suffer from moments of intense loneliness in the middle of what seems to be strenuous activity with crowds of people all around. Other people are one of the commonest barricades against loneliness behind which we seek shelter. We shield ourselves with gargantuan work loads. We duck behind emergencies, crises and deadlines (sometimes of our own making!) and try to pretend that we are far too busy to be lonely. We are deceiving ourselves. Shutting our eyes does not make the monster go away. There comes the briefest of pauses in the overcrowded schedule and the loneliness inside us reappears — no less terrible because we thought we had succeeded in camouflaging it for a while.

The fewer defences we have, the more terrible the loneliness becomes; a suit of armour cannot totally protect a knight from a battle-axe wielded by a brawny opponent, but it does offer some protection. Being busy in the middle of a crowd can't keep loneliness at bay forever, but it's a thousand times better than being housebound in a lonely flat miles from friends and family.

The sadness and emptiness of physical loneliness and social isolation make us more vulnerable to that invisible inner loneliness which assails the heart, the mind and the spirit; just as being in a bustling group at the centre of the social scene makes us temporarily less vulnerable. Noisy crowds are the cheap plastic sunglasses which some of us wear in an attempt to reduce the harsh glare of loneliness.

Evidently, being with other people, being with friends, being with a loving and closely knit family provides us with some anodyne against loneliness, but even in the best, the warmest and most loving of human groups there is no complete cure.

Whether we recognize it or not, loneliness is the symptom of spiritual starvation: just as the body is made to run on food and drink, so the soul is made to run on fellowship with the God who created it, loves it and longs for its company. What I call my inner loneliness is the warning bell which my soul is constantly ringing, a peal too deep and desperate to embellish its longing with mere words. It does not matter whether I can formulate the thought or not; it does not matter whether I can admit my need or no. The Reality is infinitely greater than my thoughts or feelings: I want God; I need God; I must find God —and nothing except a creature-to-Creator relationship with Him will cure me.

The human companions whom we love and who love us here on earth, and whose fellowship is also vital to our true eternal happiness, are invited to be our fellow guests at God's Feast: the everlasting joy of being with Christ at the Eternal Banquet is enriched and beautified beyond measure by the presence of those we love, but we must never mistake our beloved fellow guests for the Provider and Host. The Divine Repast is loveliest of all when we partake of it in loving human fellowship, but the best of human company cannot by itself provide the cure for our innermost loneliness.

In the pages that follow I have tried to offer a few suggestions which I hope and pray may help some of us to cope with various kinds of loneliness; but my own quite varied life experiences over the past five decades have led me inexorably to one conclusion: whatever our human circumstances, the only true and lasting cure for inner loneliness is a right relationship with God through His Son, Jesus Christ.

My prayer for every reader is that your loneliness will eventually end in the eternal and abundant fellowship of God's Everlasting Kingdom alongside all those whom you have loved on earth.

Lionel Fanthorpe,
CARDIFF, 1990

Alone in a Strange Town or City

This is a strange place. These are not my streets. They are familiar, yet unfamiliar. One lamp-post is like another. Fish and chip shops are the same wherever you go. So are the coffee bars, and the hamburger houses. So are the pubs, and the little corner shops. Newsagents and multiples are very much alike. When you've seen one supermarket you've seen them all. So why is this place not my place? Why do I not feel at home here? Perhaps because I have no memories of it.

I was not born here. I never played in these streets. I never ran through these parks as a child. I never took my pocket-money to that corner shop to buy my sweets from the old man in the white shop-coat who always said "Hello, Jenny," or " Hello, Peter." My mother and father never helped me fly my kite in these playing fields. This wasn't the school I went to. I didn't pass my driving test in these narrow streets, with their unexpected one way systems and their 'No Entry' signs.

My old friend Harry doesn't live on the next block. I don't know anyone here at all. Oh, yes I do though.

God is here. His Son Jesus Christ is here. The Holy Spirit is here. It doesn't matter if I have no other friends here. This is God's town. This is Christ's city.

The Holy Spirit guards these streets. He knows every inch of them. Nothing is unfamiliar to Him. I am welcome here: this is my Father's town; this city belongs to my Elder Brother. No harm can come to me here — or anywhere. All places belong to God and I belong to Him as well. He'll make sure that this is the right place for me, if I put my trust in Him. There are no strange towns. There are no strange cities. God is everywhere.

Poem

I shouldn't feel strange in my Father's town;
I mustn't let loneliness get me down.
I cannot say that I've no friends here
When the Spirit of God is always near.
It isn't the place where I was born,
But it's still my sun that paints the dawn.
It's my same old moon that shines by night,
And it's God my Father who gives them light.
However far I may have to roam
My Father's city is still my home.

Prayer

Loving and caring Heavenly Father, I am in a strange city, an unknown town, and I feel lonely and unsure of myself. I do not know my way around this place. Everything is unfamiliar. Help me to understand, loving Lord, that all the towns and cities of the earth are Yours, and that wherever I go, I am still at home because my Father is there with me. Amen.

Alone in Old Age

When I was a child, I never dreamt it would ever come to this. We were a big family then. There were plenty of relatives, friends and neighbours popping in to see us. But the years rolled on: people died; people moved away. Now I'm alone: old and alone. I feel like a character on one of those heart-breaking posters the charities put up asking for money to help lonely old people. Somehow, without noticing quite how it happened, I feel as if I've slipped out of real life. It's almost as if I've stopped being a person and turned into a prototype on a poster.

I can't remember things as well I used to. I can't think as clearly as I used to. My body feels old, frail, tired and worn out. I look in the mirror some days and I want to cry. I look at old photographs and cry, too. I look at myself as a child, as a young adult, and as I was in powerful middle age — and it makes me cry.

I used to look at old people when I was young: sometimes I laughed at them; sometimes I felt sorry for them; and sometimes I felt frightened of them. Now I know why I was frightened. They were threatening me with their wrinkles, their baldness, their bent, frail bodies and their breathlessness. They were warning me about the enemy we call Time. They were saying: "If you live long enough, you'll be like this, too!"

And now it's happened. I've joined them. I'm the sad old man on the charity poster: I've become the helpless old woman in the church magazine photograph. God help me. I am old and alone.

Wait a minute; it doesn't have to be like that. I'm only as old as I feel. All right, so I can't iron out all the wrinkles, and I can't run a 100 metres in 14 seconds any more. But old age is like any other time of life — it's what you make of it. General de Gaulle was in charge of France when he was my age. Field Marshal Radetzky was eighty-three years old when he directed the Austrian victory at Novara in 1849. There are formidable old martial arts instructors in Japan and Korea who are years older than I am, but who are still capable of beating six strong men young enough to be their grandsons. Queen Eleanor of Aquitaine successfully held Mirabeau near Poitiers against Arthur of Brittany in 1202 when she was in her eightieth year.

With God's help, I can be as active, as tough and as resolute as they were. I may be old, and I may be alone — but with the Lord's help I can still fight. My spirit, my real personality, hasn't been eroded by Time — my real self is stronger than ever, and it's been reinforced by experience. If I put my mind to it, I can do anything. The world's just as much mine to conquer as it was fifty years ago. Well done Radetzky! Congratulations Queen Eleanor! Now I'll show you what I can do — with God to guide and strengthen me!

Poem

I found a yellowed photograph, within the well-thumbed page,
A face I scarcely recognized, without one trace of age.
And yet I could remember well what those young eyes had seen
In days that vanished long ago as if they'd never been.

I gazed upon that vanished face, and wept to call it
   mine:
The mirror showed me all too well the ravages of Time,
But yet that child, so obstinate, still lives within my
   heart:
The man I was — the man I am — are not that far apart.

God, wipe the rust off this old sword, and off my
   sword-arm too,
Then help me find another task to undertake for You.
I *will* not sink beneath this weight of loneliness and
   fears —
You've helped me beat my other foes: now help me
   beat the years!

Prayer

God of all valour, Lord and Companion of the old and
the weary who try to fight on alone, please help me
now. I have many enemies, within and without. I
struggle against tiredness, pain and stiff joints. I
breathe hard as I climb the stairs. Help me, great God
of Battles, to struggle on against this loneliness and the
problems of age. Strengthen my will, so that I can push
this old body on when it doesn't want to go. Refresh
my memory, and renew my faculties. Show me a job I
can still do for you, Lord, and for others, then give me
the strength, courage and confidence to do it well. I ask
it for the sake of Him Who stumbled with exhaustion
and pain beneath His Cross, but then went on to win
the World's Greatest Victory, Jesus Christ, my Lord.
Amen.

Alone in the Country

There is one loneliness of the city and another of the country. Astronomers tell us that we live on a very small planet, yet there are places on it so wild and open that they dwarf us and lose us. There are forests and jungles that seem to go on forever. There are deserts that seem to stretch to infinity in every direction. There are oceans and seas so wide that they seem boundless to us. The space between the stars is God's country too. In those distances we are lost indeed. A person can stand in the middle of wild mountains, or wide-spreading plains and look up at the stars: it makes him or her feel insignificant and helpless, but it is also a reminder of our Father's infinite power and love. All the emptiness makes an individual feel very small and very lonely. It reminds us that we really need our Father's care, and one another's fellowship.

Out here in the great outdoors, I feel as if I was the last human being on earth — just me and the emptiness. It is an awe-inspiring place, and it makes me think.

Perhaps that is one of the reasons God gave it to us —to make us think, to help us to find our true perspective, to put ourselves in context beside Him. Perhaps the wide expanses of nature are part of our education, our preparation for Heaven. Perhaps they are there to remind us of our need for Him. All that emptiness — so much emptiness that only God can fill it.

There are other thoughts that occur to us when we are alone with nature. We are not God's only creatures. What goes on in the deepest parts of the wide oceans? What moves through the paths of the sea? How much life teems on a single leaf? How much life flourishes in one cubic centimetre of ordinary garden soil? The frogs in their pools and ponds, tiny monkeys in their arboreal havens, seagulls on craggy cliffs: all are God's creatures. St Francis with rare spiritual insight felt the bond between all that lives. Being alone with nature reminds me that although I have no human companions in this wild place, God and his birds and beasts are still here with me.

Prayer

Loving and creating Father, help us to find You in what You have made and in what You constantly sustain. Help us to look with awe at the starry heights, and to wonder at the intricacy of snowflake patterns. Reveal Your power and love in everything around us: the size of the universe, the promise of a budding flower, the delicate colour and minute detail of a butterfly's wing. Teach us to commune with nature, and through nature to commune with You, so that we never feel alone out here. Make us observant and appreciative of all that beauty and all that mystery. We ask it for the sake of Jesus, our Lord. Amen.

Alone in the World

It can happen suddenly. There is a terrible accident. Ships collide and sink. An iceberg tears a gaping rent in a hull through which the cold Atlantic pours. A plane is sabotaged by terrorists. A train is derailed. A gas boiler explodes: a tower block collapses. A whole family is wiped out except for one shocked and lonely survivor.

It can happen slowly, almost imperceptibly. The youngest child of a large family born over eighty years ago is left lonelier and lonelier by the passing years as first one older brother or sister dies and then another. Slowly the realisation dawns on that last survivor: "I am alone in the world."

It is not true. We are never alone in the world. We are the children of a Father who cannot die and leave us orphaned. We are the brothers and sisters of an Elder Brother who has already conquered death for our sakes. We belong to the great family of the Church, the People of God.

Our earthly friends and relations who have gone on before us to be with God are not lost; they have not ceased to be; they are more alive than they ever were.

They are more alive than we are now. They are enjoying such peace, light and glory in the presence of Christ, the Holy Spirit and God our Father that we cannot even begin to imagine what they are experiencing.

When Satan whispers in our inward ear that we are alone in the world, he lies abominably. The flying clouds in the blue sky are messengers from God: "Look at our beauty," they cry. "We are no accidents. Your Father made us." The raindrop trickling down your window pane brings word from God: "As surely as I flow back to the river and the sea and then return again to the clouds, so you shall flow back to the God who made and loves you. At this moment I am one lonely drop: but I shall be reunited with the countless millions of drops that have fallen before me. I cannot see the rivers and seas from this window pane. But I know that they are there, and that I shall go to them." The sun emerges, laughing, from behind the clouds. "Death?" he asks in a puzzled voice. "Loneliness? Of course not! My brightness is the thinnest, palest shadow of God's glory. Bright as I look to you, I am a very small and insignificant star among countless millions in God's universe. You look up here and think I am *the* sun. You think I am alone in your sky."

"There are millions like me out here in space — so far apart that light itself takes centuries to travel between us. I know that my brothers and sisters are shining there in their own quadrants even though vast gulfs lie between us. I am not alone. You are not alone. God never made us to be alone."

"I know that, Lord," my heart whispers, "but I still feel that I am alone. I crave human company: voices I can hear, faces I can see, hands I can clasp."

"I am here," He answers. "Your earthly senses cannot tell you that I am near, but reach for Me with the hand of faith, listen for Me with the inward ear, watch for Me with the eyes of hope, and most assuredly you shall find Me."

Prayer

Lord of Hosts, I am alone in the world. Be with me to protect me. Be my Father and my Brother. Help me to feel the presence of Your Holy Spirit, always with me, always strengthening and comforting me. Help me to pray constantly, and to listen for Your voice when I pray. Send earthly friends and neighbours to be with me as well. Grant me human companionship again. Reassure me that all those whom I have loved and lost awhile are safe with You. Tell my soul that we shall all be together again with You, in unimaginable joy forever. For the sake of Jesus, my Lord. Amen.

Alone with our Thoughts

There is an inner universe as well as an external one. The world of thought is unbelievably vast — some philosophers might argue that it is at least the equal of the material universe which the senses can observe, or even that it is greater. There may be some limits to the physical universe, but is there any limit at all to the power of thought and the distance which imagination can reach? Inside our heads is the spaceship, the magic carpet, the flying horse which will carry us further than we know how to ask.

Not long ago I acquired a much more complicated, advanced and up to date computer/word processor than the faithful old 464 which I'd used for years. The new one does semi-miraculous things with what I type into it; its impressive handbook of instructions is 624 pages long. At the moment I understand and can use less than 5% of what it can actually do for me. The human mind is infinitely more advanced and complicated than the most magnificent computer yet available. We all use only a tiny percentage of our real potential. When we are alone with our thoughts there is a whole new universe waiting inside us to be explored.

To start with there is the unknown power of the mind and especially of the will. In our present state of knowledge of the human mind we are like toddlers who have wandered into a nuclear laboratory full of buttons to press, dials to watch and levers to pull. The problem is that we don't know which levers will bring us all we've dreamed of and which ones will blow the planet away.

There are many well documented and authenticated cases of miraculous healing. We have the clue in what our Lord Himself said repeatedly during His earthly ministry: faith. "Do you believe that I can heal you?" He asked. When the miracle had happened He said "Your faith has saved you."

When Christ says that faith the size of a grain of mustard seed will move a mountain, He is not being poetic or speaking metaphorically, He is teaching us something vital about the nature of the universe and the power of the mind which God has entrusted to each one of us. When you are alone with your thoughts, you are alone with infinite power.

Prayer

Most wonderful and generous God, teach me to understand more of the mysteries of my mind. Help me to understand the power that You have entrusted to me and to use it aright. Help me, like Saint Paul of old, to think of what is good and pure, beautiful and true, noble and right. Enable me to use the precious gift of thought to learn more and more of You and Your creation, and to learn more about myself and the potential You have given me. Help me to explore my own mind with all the excitement and joy of an explorer in a strange land, so that I may never feel lonely or afraid. I ask it for Jesus' sake. Amen.

Driving Alone

Rain beats down on the screen; the wipers sweep rhythmically and monotonously over it; I am continually having to dip my lights as I meet oncoming traffic. The radio has broadcast nothing interesting for the last two hours, and it's difficult to hear anyway against the fan blowing hot air on to the inside of the screen to stop it from misting over. I am bored. I am lonely, and I am not enjoying the drive. I wish I'd bought a few new cassette tapes for the player, but I haven't any with me that I want to listen to.

This peculiar loneliness of the long distance driver, whether in a car or a lorry, is a phenomenon of the twentieth century. During the brief glories of the coaching age, the passengers were far too crowded and uncomfortable to feel lonely. The solitary modern driver in his comfortable prison on wheels has different problems.

The smoothness and comfort are deceptive. This little steel and glass box is cruising at seventy miles an hour. An impact at this speed would probably be fatal both for me and whoever I hit: that's a massive responsibility. I must keep alert. I must anticipate all the time. At one level of my mind, I'm concentrating hard. It's the other level that's bored and lonely.

I spend so much of my waking, working life driving alone. I ought to be able to put all those hours to better use. I've had more than enough work for today: I'm not going to try to plan tomorrow's business schedules: I need something more interesting, more entertaining than that. I want to use this driving time doing something real, something positive. Perhaps instead of those endless music tapes, and popular abridged novels and stories on cassettes, I could get hold of something really deep and worthwhile. What about recording a few chapters of St John's Gospel for myself to play over and think about? What about buying a cassette of something by C. S. Lewis? Instead of thinking about this time as a vacuum, a negative sort of space between calls, a desert or an ocean between home and work, why don't I start looking forward to it as my thinking time, the time when I'm really alive, really doing something worthwhile? This could be an ideal time for praying, talking to God and listening to God. This could be an ideal time for slow, careful self-examination: I can ask myself who I am, what I'm here on earth for, and where I'm going. This is a time when I can think deeply about my relationship with God, and with His other children, my brothers and sisters on this planet.

Prayer

Lord of this road, and of all roads, Lord of the Road of Life itself, help me to use my driving time in the best possible way: to pray quietly, to think deeply and to drive carefully, for the sake of Christ my Lord. Amen.

Hoping for a Visit

When we are ill or infirm, elderly or housebound, visits are worth more to us than our friends will ever know. The milkman, the postman, the newspaper delivery boy, the lady next door just popping in to see if we're all right — they all mean so much to us. The Vicar, a social worker, the man to read the gas meter, our home help, the man from Meals on Wheels — each one has a massive contribution to make to our lives. We just sit alone, or lie alone, and long for a visit.

We are tired of radio. Our eyes will not let us read much. The television has nothing to offer. Putting a record on an old gramophone, or fiddling with a cassette tape recorder seems to be more bother than it's worth some days! What I want is a visit. I just want to see one real live human being who actually cares enough about me to call to see me.

Some days there's a very long wait.

Some days no-one comes at all.

Sometimes I'm lucky to get two visits a week.

I am very, very lonely indeed. What can I do about it?

First, I can pray. I can tell God my Father how miserable and lonely I am because no-one comes to see me, and I can ask Him to send someone. I know that He cares, and I know that prayer is real and effective. I also know that I must never give up when I pray. Jesus told a wonderful story about an unjust judge and a poor widow. The widow never gave up, and at last the unjust judge gave in and settled the case for her. If even an unjust judge gives in in the end, how much more readily will God my Father, Who loves me very much and is perfect Justice, come to my rescue now? I know He will if I ask Him. I'll knock at the doors of Heaven with my prayers until I do get an answer. I'll ask my father until I do receive . I'll pray the prayer of faith, and I'll keep on praying.

Second, I'll find something to do that will take my mind off it. Am I well enough to get as far as my kitchen and make a nice cup of tea? Can I grill myself a slice of toast? If I'm not able to get out of bed, what happy memories can I call up while I lie here? If my legs aren't much use to me now, I can still make my thoughts run, jump and skip. Can I remember my school days, sixty years ago and more? There, I've covered all those years in a flash. What was that game I always used to like best? The one with the skipping rope, wasn't it? Or was it a hoop? Parts of it have faded, but I'll make up the bits I've forgotten. Then what about the fun we used to have at Christmas, and on birthdays? Those games we used to play at our parties? The day the man came with his puppet show?

How I enjoyed that old Punch and Judy! What a fuss Punch made when the crocodile got hold of his nose! I'm laughing just to think of it again.

Third, is there anything I can do about it myself? Is there any action I can take, however limited I am these days, which will help to bring a visit nearer? God expects us to do what we can for ourselves as well as to pray for help. The sailors always used to say: "Trust in God, but steer away from the rocks." How can I steer away from these rocks of loneliness while I lie here waiting for a visit? Is there someone I can 'phone? Is there anyone I can think of who might have a minute or two to drop in and see me?

Poem and Prayer

I long for a visit; I need company;
Dear Lord, in Your mercy, send someone to me
The Vicar, the postman, a friend on the 'phone —
Dear Lord, send me *someone*: I feel so alone.
The milkman, the butcher, the newspaper boy—
The sound of a footstep would fill me with joy.
The ring of the doorbell; the rap of a hand;
A smile through this window would be something grand.
I know You are here, Lord, and here to the end,
But please would You send me just *one* human friend?
Although my blessed Saviour means all things to me,
I long for a friend with a face I can see. Amen.

Ill, in Pain and Alone

The pain seems so much worse when there's no-one to talk to. I feel so weak and ill that I can hardly bear to be inside this body. The pain just won't stop. It won't let me rest. I can't think against it. The whole of what used to be my world has collapsed into a whirlpool of weakness and a maelstrom of pain.

Did You feel like this on the Cross, Lord Jesus? Your suffering must have been infinitely worse than this. You more than anyone can understand what I'm going through now. You're so much stronger than I am, Lord. Please, please help me. Please, please make me well again. Let me recover some of my strength, and please take this endless pain away.

Being alone makes it so much worse, Lord. I want someone with me. When I can think at all, my thoughts are filled with fear. I want someone near me, to reassure me, to comfort me, to care about me. Please, Lord Jesus, send someone to help me.

Slowly, almost imperceptibly, the waves of pain begin to calm down, as the storm calmed down on Galilee so long ago, Lord, when You told it to be still. Slowly, almost imperceptibly, a few strands of strength creep back into my exhausted limbs.

Very, very gradually, I begin to feel just a tiny bit better — and, oh, how wonderful that smallest of improvements is! Please keep on helping me, Lord. I need You so much, and I'm no longer afraid once I remember that You're with me.

Poem

A sinking ship of weariness, upon a sea of pain,
The waves will overwhelm me if they strike my craft
again.
The sickness and the weariness, exhaustion and
despair —
I wouldn't feel so lost if there was someone here to
care.
Lord, speak to me, to reassure, to comfort and console.
I feel as if the waves of death are breaking round my
soul.
You suffered far, far more than this, upon the Cross for
me:
O suffering God, help me endure my lesser Calvary.

Prayer

Most merciful God, You know so much more about suffering than I do. Please have mercy on me and heal me. Please take away my pain, my sickness, my weakness and my weariness. Send someone to help me, Lord, someone to care, someone to comfort me. Send me a smiling face, and a warm, gentle hand. Send me a loving, tender voice to speak words of healing and peace. I ask it for the sake of the Prince of Peace and the Master of Healing, Jesus Christ my Lord. Amen.

Living Alone

I can't grumble. It's a nice place, really. It's got every facility. I'm warm, dry and comfortable. I've got a decent bed, a roof over my head, a nice little cooker and a kettle that boils fast when I want a drop of tea. There's my radio and my television. I've even got a record player. Some people would call it luxury. I've got enough regular income to meet my needs, and I can manage a few luxuries now and then. I enjoyed the coach trip to the sea last month. That was good. But it's the coming home to an empty place that's so hard to take. Yes, I know it's not isolated. There are neighbours, of course. We say "Good morning," or "Good afternoon," as we pass, or if we run into one another at the shops — but that's as far as it goes: we're only acquaintances, not friends, not proper companions. I do miss having someone to share my home with me.

God never intended us to live alone: husbands and wives, parents and children, grandparents in the chimney corner — extended families helping one another, living together as a team — that was the Original Plan, I'm sure of it. Somewhere along the road society has lost its way. If we're ever going to cure this social disease called 'living alone' we've got to have a family revolution. We need each other. We need to be together. We need real family communities again.

Still, that doesn't solve my immediate problem. I've got to cope with what I've got until I can find a way to improve things, or until God my Father improves them for me.

First of all, I must count my blessings; I must thank God for all the good things. Then I must pray regularly and often. I know God my Father is here; so I'm not really living alone, am I? How can I be lonely? Jesus Christ my Lord is the Head of this little home. The Holy Spirit, the Comforter, is here to comfort and strengthen me as well. I've got the best Company in the universe living here with me, and as long as I can keep that clearly in mind, I'll take no harm. I never come home to an empty house — God dwells here with me. When I go out, He accompanies me. When I come home He's here to welcome me.

Prayer

Most loving Lord, best of all possible Companions, help me always to remember that You are here with me. This place is never empty: God my Father is always here. Make me ever more aware of Your radiant and wonderful Presence. Dwell not only in my home but in my heart. Fill my dwelling, Lord, and fill my life. Let me be Your living temple, and shine through me, so that in spite of all my many weaknesses and imperfections, others may see You in my life and in my home, and, seeing You here, may come to know and love You, Whom to know and love is life abundant and eternal. I ask it for the sake of Jesus Christ my Lord, Who entered many poor homes during His earthly ministry, and richly blessed them. Amen.

Praying Alone

There is all the difference in the universe — the spiritual or physical universe — between praying in a group, praying with a partner, and praying entirely alone. In communal prayer of the kind we say together in Church we are visiting God on a coach tour; when we pray with a partner, or in a small family group, we are sharing a taxi to the steps of His Throne; when we pray alone we are walking along a secret short-cut —tip-toeing up the back stairs to Heaven. To pray alone is to be alone with God — the most precious and intimate relationship which any human being can ever aspire to.

You . . . me . . . one of His creatures can actually dare to speak alone and in complete confidence to Him: our God, our Father, our Maker. It is the most breathtaking and awe-inspiring of all thoughts. Daring to approach God alone is more daring than climbing Everest alone, swimming the Channel without an escort boat, or sailing single-handedly around the world. *We tiny, sinful creatures dare to approach God and talk to Him.* And we can find that courage because He has not only issued an open and perpetual invitation to us, He has actually encouraged us to come to have fellowship with Him. Christ, His Son, has made it unequivocally clear to us that our Father enjoys our company and loves nothing more than having us with Him. He wants us to share His Eternal and Abundant Life.

That is the spirit in which Christ invites us to approach God. Come with repentance. Come with a deep and sincere longing to be with your Father. And never be afraid to come secretly and alone. There is a permanent and guaranteed welcome for each son and daughter, whether we use the coach service of our local Church, the taxi-ride with family and close friends, or the quiet walk through secret ways.

Poem

A world of millions like me, and yet I kneel alone
In silent prayer, Great Father God, before the
    Heavenly throne.
A world of millions like me, Lord — each daughter,
every son —
Yet in Your boundless love, dear God, you know us
    every one.
Oh strange and wondrous privilege, Great Father of us
    all,
That You invite us each to pray — and listen when we
    call.

Prayer

Most loving Father, I have come to You quite alone to reveal the most secret thoughts and longings of my innermost heart. Hear my joyful praise and my humble repentance in this solemn, silent moment, and listen to these my most private and deepest prayers and intercessions, for the sake of Christ my Lord. Amen.

The Lonely Academic

Marlowe made Faust say, "I'll burn my books!" Some days I think I know how he felt! I get so lonely here in my ivory tower. They tell me that there are people out there who envy me. We all envy one another, I suppose. Right now I'd rather be the woman scrubbing the college step than the learned doctor writing this research paper. At this moment I'd rather be that assistant gardener under my window sweeping up the leaves and putting them in his barrow. The doorstep is real. The bucket is real. The scrubbing brush is real. The leaves and the broom and the barrow are real. I just manipulate abstract concepts: my brother and sister down there are doing something positive, real and solid.

I wonder why I chose this life. Did I really choose it, or did it just happen to me? My father was a professor here before he retired. Leather armchairs and oak panels were something I grew up with — and books, of course: endless, endless rows of books. What am I missing up here behind the old grey stones and the ivy? Business, commerce, politics, manufacturing, selling, playing games, watching soap operas on television? Do I need any of those things? I miss people: real, solid, honest, flesh and blood human beings who can't read Greek and who think that Differential Calculus was a Roman general.

Yet a man has to do what a man has to do, as the hero inevitably said in those old westerns I used to watch when I was a boy; it's the same for the mountaineer who said he had to climb the mountain just because it was there. *If you've got the sort of mind that can manipulate abstract concepts you have to do it.* The trouble is today that we've all diverged so far along our own specialisms that we can hardly talk to one another about those concepts any more — let alone try to explain them to our brothers and sisters out there. There are probably only twenty people in the world who really understand what this research of mine is about, and most of them are in other universities in other countries. I almost wish I could have lived at the time when the sum of human knowledge was small enough for everyone to learn it all. Today's academic life is increasingly lonely.

Still, God knows what I'm doing. He knows infinitely more about my programme than all twenty of us top specialists put together. He designed every abstraction that I've ever heard of, and countless millions that our little human brains haven't yet got to grips with. There is no thought in my head which He doesn't fully understand, and there never can be. Even if I know something so esoteric that no-one else on earth shares it with me, God does. My remotest abstraction never takes me beyond the reach of His Infinite Divine Mind.

Poem

Lord of infinity, God of the microscope,
Maker of all things, Sustainer and Guide:
Wavelengths and languages,
Concepts and principles —
Loving and fatherly, here at man's side.

God of the galaxies, painter of sunsets,
Sculptor of snowflakes, Who taught fish to swim,
Master and Mentor, both Saviour and Father,
Wisdom and Virtue are Aspects of Him.

Master of aeons, both timeless and changeless,
Lord of All Being and all that can be:
This is our God Who once told His disciples:
"Suffer the children to come unto Me."

Prayer

Omnipotent, omniscient and omnipresent Lord,
Creator of mind and thought, guide me through these
difficult abstractions and help me to contend with the
loneliness of this academic life. Help me always to
understand that all True Knowledge comes from You,
and, if used aright, will always lead back to You. Teach
me how to be a person — a complete human being
—as well as an academic, so that I too may enjoy
friends and fellowship. Amen.

The Lonely Walk

Walking is a wonderful gift, yet how often we take it for granted. Sometimes we grumble when we have to walk because we have no cycle to ride, no car to drive, no train or bus waiting at the station. Sometimes we complain about having to walk in intense heat, or to plod through muddy fields, or to protect our faces against the rain, sleet, snow and hail. How sadly limited we should feel if we were no longer able to walk: let us thank God for good legs, and enjoy walking whenever we get the chance. Pray for everyone in a wheelchair, or struggling along gamely on crutches.

Walking can be so automatic that it gives us a wonderful opportunity to think while we are getting the benefit of the exercise as well. Walking is symbolic of our whole path through life. We can make good use of a quiet, lonely walk by meditating on the meaning of life, thinking over what we've done so far, and planning ahead. We can pray as we walk. We can use the time and the quiet peace of the lonely walk to intercede for others, especially those who are themselves unable to walk.

The more slowly we walk, the more we can see. A quiet walk alone is an opportunity to observe everything around us: trees, birds, flowers, insects, stones and grass, the colours of the sky, the cloud formations — even the moon and stars when we walk alone at night.

Poem

I love to walk alone and think
Between the earth and sky,
To feel the grass beneath my feet
And scan the mountains high.

I love to walk alone and think
Between the beach and tide,
And wonder as I scan the waves
About the Other Side.

I love to walk alone and think
Of years that used to be.
I wonder if the child I meet
Could really have been me.

I love to walk alone and think
Of all that lies before:
The joy that Christ has promised us
Upon the Other Shore.

Prayer

Loving heavenly Father, Perfect Companion for my
walk through life, be with me every step of the way.
Guard me and guide, Lord of the Journey. Never let me
fall. Encourage and strengthen me when the way is
steep and rough, and bring me safely home, for
Christ's sake. Amen.

Solving a Problem Alone

There are times when something we have to cope with is difficult if not impossible to share. It may involve some third party whose confidence we must not betray. We then find ourselves unable to answer the perfectly reasonable and kindly meant questions of other friends except in a vague or oblique manner. For example, a close friend or relative with marital problems has confided something and asked for help and advice. There is no-one with whom we can share the problem other than God himself in our silent prayers.

It may be that we have some secret personal problem which cannot be confided because of the unfair and unreasonable weight which it would place upon other human shoulders: we feel that we must bear it alone, solve it alone. Only God can help us.

Occasionally it is our pride, that prevents us from seeking help. What is secret is not the problem itself —that may be something quite commonplace — but our reluctance to admit that we can't solve it. Especially in a field where we have (or we fondly imagine we have a reputation for having) some special knowledge or expertise, we may find that a simple answer eludes us, and we don't feel that we can ask for help without admitting our ignorance in an area where we are supposed to be knowledgeable.

Pride and a departure from the simple, plain truth at the beginning of the matter are the most common causes of this dilemma. We all know how it starts. Someone says during a discussion, "What do you think of Hargreaves' Postulate in connection with this problem?" The insidious temptation is to nod sagely and mutter something like, "It's a most interesting argument and could well be relevant here." What we ought to do, of course, is to admit frankly that we haven't the remotest idea what it was that Hargreaves postulated, or why, or when! We don't even know who Hargreaves was, yet everybody else seems to, so we don't like to confess our ignorance! The next thing that happens is that we're asked to lead a discussion on Hargreaves' wretched Postulate, or deliver a paper on it, or write an article about him for the Church Magazine. The lonely problem then is to find something out about him without disclosing how little we knew in the first place, and thus revealing the depth of our silly pride and pomposity.

Fortunately for all sinners, even the most pompous and proud, Jesus understands. He's trodden the road ahead of us. He never succumbed to that particularly tricky little temptation, yet it was laid cunningly before Him during His earthly ministry. He can understand us perfectly and forgive us completely when we take that lonely problem to Him in prayer.

So, once again, with absolute assurance, we may turn to Christ for an answer. The impossible, lonely problem, that one we feel unable to share with anyone on earth — for whatever reason — may safely be shared with Christ, Who, having been here on earth before us, knows all the answers and is more than willing, is eager, in fact, to help us through our solitary difficulties. Tell Him. Tell Him now. He will undoubtedly help you through it. Not only will He provide the only worthwhile answer, He will give you the extra strength you need to put that answer into effect.

Poem

I cannot solve this thing alone
And yet I dare not share it;
The problem is too hard for me —
One mind alone can't bear it.
"Come unto Me," the Saviour said.
"My way, you know, is best.
Tell me, My child, what troubles you,
And I will give you rest."

Prayer

Loving Saviour, Sharer of all burdens and Solver of all problems, help me with this difficulty which I cannot share with any earthly friend. I cannot cope with it alone anymore, and so I bring it to You in perfect trust. Amen.

The Loneliness of Bereavement

"The Rubaiyat of Omar Khayyam" dates from the eleventh century. Omar was an astronomer and poet who lived in Persia, and his sad but beautiful verses contain his meditations on the mysteries and meaning of life. There was, he wrote, a door to which he found no key. There was a veil through which he could not see. It was the door of death, the veil of bereavement.

His courage and fortitude were immense: his conclusions were wrong. Death is the ultimate challenge as far as this world is concerned. Omar faced that challenge head on with only the flimsiest of weapons: the simple pursuit of earthly pleasure. It is about as effective to meet the grimly massive challenge of death with that defence as it is to flick the corner of a handkerchief into the face of a charging rhinoceros. You cannot help but admire the courage of a man who acknowledges the presence of the charging rhinoceros and uses his handkerchief against it rather than nothing at all, but you cannot help wondering whether there were better weapons he might have found if he had looked further for them.

Wollaston, an eminent early nineteenth century chemist and geologist who gave his name to the mineral known as wollastonite, used the defence of scientific detachment and the true researcher's curiosity. Dying of a brain tumour which had paralysed both his hands, he still continued with great courage and fortitude to dictate his scientific notes until the day he died.

Samson, Judge of Israel, a blinded captive in the Philistine Temple of Dagon, wanted to die exalting in the glory of triumphant revenge as he brought that same temple crashing down on himself and thousands of his enemies.

The true Viking warrior faced death sword in hand, determined to reach Valhalla — the Viking paradise — by dying bravely in battle, or sailing there in a blazing ship.

There are many brave men and women who have faced death, and who are facing death even at this moment, by combining the quiet resignation of Omar Khayyam, the intellectual detachment of Wollaston, and the sheer physical courage of warriors like Samson or Eric Bloodaxe. A hero is no less a hero facing lingering terminal pain in a hospice than facing axe and sword on the field of honour.

Yet all their defences yield at the last, and death storms the citadel.

What then?

What of those who love them so much, and are left behind to mourn? How can they cope with the loneliness of bereavement?

Our earthly defences against bereavement are very similar to the defences we try to use against death itself. We become resigned to it, and we try to find pleasant things to do to take our minds off it. We find some great cause — scientific or otherwise — and we follow that 'greater' thing with almost fanatical zeal. We fight, literally or metaphorically, to try to overcome whatever it was that caused the bereavement: we raise funds for the medical researchers working in that area; we devote ourselves to a campaign to improve safety in some special field. Like our defences against death, these defences also fail. They never satisfy completely. They never bridge the chasm. They never fill the aching void. They never fly us across the gulf.

There is one answer and one answer alone. It is the answer to death, and it is the answer to bereavement.

It is Christ

We can try anything and everything else, but to no avail. Without Christ death wins. Without Christ bereavement scours us to the bone like a wire brush dipped in caustic soda. Without Christ we are already effectively dead, although we are still walking around and talking, going through the pathetic puppet show of pretending to be a human being.

What is it that Christ does for us?

He changes everything concerning death and bereavement: no pretending; no papering over the cracks; no avoiding of the grim and the terrible. Christ stands and faces the monster, faces it with the only weapon that can destroy it, faces it with supreme strength and courage — and brings it crashing down: defeated and destroyed forever.

That is exactly what Christ does for us at unimaginable cost to Himself

Death appears to be so terrible and final a reality when viewed from the standpoint of earth that only the Ultimate Reality of Christ can unmask it for the hideous impostor it is. God is Life, Abundant and Eternal Life. Christ His Son is the Bringer of that Life to us and all whom we love. He has the key to Omar's locked door. His are the Hands that rend the veil through which the Persian poet could not see. It is by His Cross that we cross the Great Gulf. His death is our life. His Resurrection heals our bereavement. Because He lives forever, we shall live forever. Because He loves us forever, those whom we have lost from this world will be with us again with Him in unimaginable and unending joy. Life is the nature of Christ, and Life is the Gift of Christ. In the darkest and loneliest corner of the agony of bereavement, Christ lights the Candle of Hope. It is a sure and certain hope. Nothing can extinguish it, for God Himself has kindled its Eternal Flame.

Poem

You will never be forgotten. I shall always remember
    you.
And each time I remember, I shall pray for you.
I shall plead with Christ to take especial care of you
Because I love you so much.

I have a desperate longing to see you again
And to be with you forever in His Kingdom of Light
    and Joy,
Where there is no more death, and no more loneliness,
Because I love you so much.

Until then, I shall try for His sake, and for yours,
To do the best I can with the rest of my life,
To fly your flag and wield your sword as if you were
    still here,
Because I love you so much.

Be there beside Him to open the Gate for me when I
    come.
And pray for me meanwhile — those stronger, better
    prayers
Which Angels know. Remember me, as I remember
    you,
Because I love you so much.

Prayer

Most loving, caring Lord, You wept for your friend
Lazarus long ago. You understand this terrible grief,
pain and loneliness I feel now. You love those we have
lost even more than we do. Comfort me in my
loneliness and take care of all those I love so much who
are now with You. Re-unite us in Your Perfect Time
and in Your Perfect Place, for Your Name's Sake.
Amen.

The Loneliness of Keeping a Secret

Secrets can be incredibly heavy things to bear. There are so many temptations to lay them down, yet those temptations must be resisted at all costs. For the true, sincere and dedicated Priest, the Seal of the Confessional is absolute: those are the secrets he carries to the grave with him. You do not have to be in Holy Orders to find yourself occasionally in a parallel situation to that of the Father Confessor. The close friend or loving relative confides something very important to you, and the burden of secrecy is firmly welded to your shoulders. It is a matter of ethics, of basic morality. The secret has become part of you. It is inseparable from your integrity. It also has the power to isolate you and make you very lonely indeed. We should, therefore, be as careful as we can about what secrets we are prepared to take on board.

Prayer

Lord of every Holy Secret, to Whom all things are known, and by Whom all mysteries are fully understood, help me to bear the secrets of those who trust me faithfully and well. Protect me from all temptation to reveal what I know, or even to reveal that I know anything at all. Let no vain pride that comes from owning secrets make me boast of their possession. Prevent the heavy loneliness of secrecy from overwhelming me. Let no offer of favour, gain or advancement, nor any fear of penalty nor pain, tempt me to reveal what I have promised to keep in trust for another. I ask it for the sake of Jesus Christ, my Lord, with whom all secrets are safe forever. Amen.

The Loneliness of Language Barriers

I hear what you say, but I can understand little or nothing of it. We cannot communicate because we have no common language. You seem like a good person, kind and potentially a friend, but this barrier of language comes between us and makes me lonely.

Is there an international, universal language which we can use instead? Can I draw a picture of what I'm trying to say? Can we smile? Can we shake hands? Can I offer you food, drink, or shelter as a gesture or friendship? Can our generosity speak when words cannot?

The worst language barrier is the language our selfishness speaks, which makes it almost impossible for us to understand the language of God, or to hear the cries of people in need. It allows us only a very limited vocabulary: the first person singular nominative pronoun 'I' and the verb 'want'. Any language in the world is better than that one. Only one person speaks it, and that person will allow no one to translate or interpret. It is a wall as well as a language, and there is broken glass and barbed wire at the top. It will not let us out, and no one can get in — no one except Christ, Who does not feel the glass and barbed wire because of the other, far deeper wounds He received on our behalf long ago. He can communicate. He can interpret. He can translate.

He can transcend the barrier of our selfishness and teach us to speak another, sweeter tongue. He can break through the loneliness of that barrier, if only we will ask Him. Eager as He is to help us, He will do nothing without our consent. He Who controls the universe will do nothing to damage the freedom of the weakest human will. He on Whose smallest errands the mightiest Archangels speed with joy will not push open the flimsiest human door, unless the house-holder bids Him enter.

Poem

"I want," it cried, that tyrant voice within,
"I want the world's delights, and every sin.
I want all things for me, for me alone,
Each piece of treasure, gold and precious stone.
I want ... I want ... I want ... " it cried and cried.
None understood it, but the Crucified.
"Your wants are death," He said. "Come here and live.
Stop crying out your wants, and learn to give.
Here in My Kingdom every want shall cease —
My gifts are endless joy, and life and peace."

Prayer

Lord of all languages, Master of every tongue, help me to overcome the loneliness and frustration of earthly language barriers. Above all teach me Your Language of Love, the true Language of Heaven, and rid me of that foul and isolating language of selfishness, which left to myself I speak so readily. I ask it for the sake of Christ my Lord. Amen.

The Loneliness of a Minority Opinion

There are several variations on the old Yorkshire adage: "Everyone's daft except for thee and me, and sometimes I wonder about thee!" Most humour has elements of underlying truth and seriousness. The absolute certainty that we and we alone are right may well be spiced with humour in the north country joke but when it leads to bigotry, prejudice and fanaticism the philosophical steel protrudes starkly through the velvet glove of the humour. Of course, if an opinion has been carefully, thoughtfully and objectively reached, if it is held so strongly — as strongly as the faith of a martyred saint — that the rest of the world and every other aspect of life pale into insignificance beside it, then it is the kind of certainty that may rightly be held against all opposition and all obstacles.

Even Oliver Cromwell — not a man whom most historians categorized as liberal, permissive, progressive or vacillating — once wrote to a colleague, "I implore you to consider ... whether you might be wrong." When we have made every possible allowance for the opinions of others, and when we have taken Cromwell's advice and considered very carefully whether we might be wrong, and when all our consideration and deliberation has left us unshaken in our belief that we are right, then, as we stand by our opinion we may find ourselves in a lonely and tiny minority — even a minority of one.

The man or woman who is able to stand fearlessly for what he or she believes to be truth may, of course, be right. There was a time when it was neither safe nor easy to proclaim your belief that the earth was a sphere. In the story of the Emperor's New Clothes, when a great many people who should have known better were going along with the widely expressed view that the Emperor's new clothes were beautiful, it would have taken massive courage to be the one voice that said that the Emperor had no clothes at all.

Standing by your faith, standing by your beliefs, standing by what you sincerely hold to be the truth when you are under pressure on every side to change that view takes immense courage. H. G. Wells told a story called "The Valley of the Blind" in which only one man in the community could see. This made him so unpopular with the blind inhabitants of the valley that they wanted to blind him rather than listen to him. In the Platonic account of the prisoners in the cave who see not reality but the distorted shadows of unreal objects cast on the wall of their cave, it is suggested that if one escaped and found out the truth, should he return and tell the others they would kill him. There is a cherished security in orthodoxy, in 'received common sense'. The pioneering thinker, philosopher or theologian who tries to share new ideas with rigid orthodoxy soon finds himself under massive pressure to conform.

The brave and resolute upholder of pure old faith and tradition in a world which is riddled with doubts, uncertainties and intellectual novelties is also brought under massive pressure to abandon the beliefs of his youth and to go along with contemporary modifications and re-interpretations of what he has always believed. Whether we are innovators, or whether we are defenders of the grand old traditions, defending a minority opinion can be a lonely and thankless task.

It is integrity that matters. I am responsible to God only for what I truly believe. You are responsible to God only for what you truly believe. If when we search our hearts we can say with total honesty: "This is my real faith;" if we can say, with a great reformer of old: "Here I stand: I can do no other," then we have done all that we can do to follow the path of intellectual honesty. It is always possible that we shall ultimately be shown to be wrong, but at least we shall have the satisfaction of being honestly wrong. The loneliness of the man or woman who sincerely holds a minority opinion is an embattled loneliness — sometimes a bitter loneliness. Yet it is a loneliness which Christ our Lord shared against all the received wisdom of the Jewish leaders of His day. His was the loneliness of being right when all the disciples forsook Him and fled. His was the utter and terrible loneliness expressed in the cry from the cross. Yet through the crucible of the loneliness of the minority opinion Christ our Lord rose to glorious and eternal victory.

Poem

Dear Lord, if I am right, and all the world is wrong,
Help me to stand alone, and to be strong.
Let fear depart; let truth and right prevail —
Come storm and tempest, earthquake, flood and hail.
If I am right, God help me to stand fast
Against all odds, although I am the last.

Help me reflect, great Lord of truth and love,
Fount of all wisdom pouring from above.
Help me consider, think and think again,
Regard with care the thoughts of other men.
Help me examine all that I believe —
Always be open new truth to receive.

Dear Lord, if I am wrong, then grant me grace
To turn and seek Thee in some different place.
Give me the courage and the strength that turns
And turns again if some new truth it learns.
Thou art the Steadfast Star, seeking and sought
By which our fragile vessels come to Port.

Prayer

Lord of all truth, Who alone knowest the meaning and
nature of all things, and in Whom is eternal and infinite
wisdom, grant us the grace to use the minds that Thou
hast given us to explore the universe and its mysteries
open-mindedly and to form honest opinions. Grant us
the courage that Christ displayed during His earthly
ministry that we may always hold to what we
sincerely believe to be the truth. Amen.

The Loneliness of Poverty

Our Lord Himself blessed the poor in the course of the Sermon on the Mount, which contains some of the most beautiful spiritual truths ever revealed to mankind.

There is no blame and no stigma attached to simple poverty. Saint Francis — one of the most Christ-like holy men ever to walk the earth — sought it out deliberately, and honoured it by sharing it. Many of those who have controlled least of this world's goods have been the finest and richest characters in history.

Yet poverty has a peculiar loneliness attached to it; invisible tethers limit the movements of the poor; unseen walls keep them inside very restricted areas; there is so much that a poor man feels unable to do. The loneliness of poverty is the loneliness of being unable to afford to go where others go; to be unable to find the 'bus fare, the train fare, or the cost of the hotel room.

The loneliness of poverty is saying no to an invitation you'd love to accept because you have nothing fit to wear. The loneliness of poverty is being unable to join in the sports activity because you can't afford the basic equipment or the price of admission to the sports centre.

The loneliness of poverty is being unable to write to old friends because stamps and envelopes are expensive. The loneliness of poverty is not being able to afford a telephone. The loneliness of poverty is longing for a pet and not having enough money to feed one. The loneliness of poverty is having to live in a run-down part of the inner city where some of your friends dare not venture to visit you — especially after dark. Christ our Lord was born in a stable, and laid in a manger. He often said that he had nowhere to lay his head — even the foxes and birds had more luxurious homes than He did. Living as a village carpenter at Nazareth meant living in poverty. Jesus knew the sights, the sounds, the smells and the tastes of poverty in first century Palestine. He knows all about the loneliness of the poor today. He is concerned. He is involved. He suffers with them, as he suffered with them in Galilee during His earthly ministry. He is the Companion of the lonely poor. He is the Friend of the lonely poor. He is the Saviour of the lonely poor. He is the God of the lonely poor.

Prayer

Lord of the lonely poor, grant us Thine aid. Strengthen us in our weakness. Feed our hunger. Quench our thirst. Clothe us and give us warmth. Heal our sickness. End our poverty. Teach the rich to share with us, and teach us to share with one another. Help us to overcome all difficulties, and to give You our praise, however dark the way may be. For the sake of Him Who loved the poor, and died that we might live, Jesus Christ our Lord. Amen.

The Loneliness of Power

I remember what it was like years ago as an ordinary member of the work-team. It was possible to have friends then. No-one was afraid to be seen talking to you. You weren't suspicious of people's motives. Is this man genuine or does he want something? My memory may be deceiving me, but we all seemed to want roughly the same things in those days. Then that first promotion opportunity came along: I thought Charlie and I had been reasonably good friends until then — two candidates and one promotion opport-unity. I thought I had the better claim, too. I'd been there longer than he had ... Oh, well! It was over twenty years ago. It shouldn't matter now, but I still recall the bitterness of the disappointment when he got it. There was no stopping me then until I'd got promotion somewhere else. It became a sort of obses-sion. I'm not really sure what I was trying to prove: I just had this irresistible drive to get on, to climb the ladder. Every rung you reached just opened up a more tantalising view of the column of rungs above it. So it went on for years. Finally I got there.

The crazy, ironic thing was that society had changed somehow during the years that I was climbing. The view from the top of the hill wasn't anything like the view you got of the top of the hill while you were still looking up at it from the valley floor! In the days when I was climbing, being the Boss meant something. When I finally got to be the Boss, I found out that the whole thing was an image, a fake. There wasn't any real power there to be wielded, at least not in my line of work. It was all committees and consultations; advisory meetings and training programmes; government regulations and professional associations' recommendations. It wasn't my scene at all. There was no satisfaction in it. My image of a Boss was a real, independent decision maker: a combination of Robin Hood, Captain Flint of "The Black Swan", Garibaldi and Al Capone — with just a touch of Charlemagne, Louis XIV or Caesar Augustus to provide a little nobility and dignity. So I'd exchanged all the good, old, genuine friendship of being one of the lads for a powerless paper crown, a desk full of bureaucratic rubbish, and the atmosphere of loneliness and suspicion that inevitably surrounds the man or woman at the top. Not a very profitable exchange!

Even if some of your power is real, and it's not all hollow and illusory, it's still very lonely. Holding the top job, the captaincy, the headship, the bishopric, the managing directorship is never quite what you'd hoped it would be. All it does is isolate you. Almost everyone you meet is either offering advice or asking favours: most of the advice is dubious because the self-appointed advisers haven't got access to even half your data; and the favours usually can't be granted because you haven't got the necessary power to make decisions in those areas!

Poem

"Ambition is a grievous fault," so Shakespeare's
    Roman said,
And Caesar answered grievously — ambition left him
    dead.

It isn't done with knives today; it's done with words instead.

My thoughts were bitter when I felt unjustly over-passed:

It spurred me on to fight and climb. I reached the top at last.

Upon the highest mountain peak, there blows the coldest blast.

"Have what you want: and pay for it," the Chinese proverb ran.

The price of power is loneliness: pick up that bill who can.

Is life not better on the plains, alongside brother man?

Yet some must wield the rod of power, if ought is to be done.

The Moon is Mistress of the Night; the Day obeys the Sun.

God shield me from the loneliness of being such a one!

Prayer

Almighty and everlasting God, Essence of Power, and absolute Ruler of all things, You understand power as no earthly mind can ever understand it. Show those of us who wield it how to wield it in accordance with Your Will. The greatest of us have so many flaws and weaknesses, and the weakest of us have powers we do not realise or use properly. Never let power isolate us, Lord. Keep us close to You, and close to our brothers and sisters. Show us that all power derives from You, and help us always to use it aright, for Jesus' sake. Amen.

The Loneliness of Unemployment

My common sense tells me it's not my fault. My reason tells me there's nothing wrong with me. But it's the irrational feeling that hurts: I feel rejected; I feel unwanted; I feel curiously redundant — in every sense of the word. Everyone that counts — my family, my real friends — they're doing all they can to help and reinforce me, to reassure me that it's not my fault, that I'm not to blame. But I can't help feeling inferior and inadequate in some way. There's a terrible inner loneliness to being unemployed. I know that if there are only twenty jobs going and fifty people want them, thirty of us are going to be unemployed, and there's no disgrace in being one of the thirty. Knowing it at that sort of cold, detached, intellectual level is one thing: the way it actually feels, as an emotion, is different again. I want a job. I really do want a job. I am not lazy. I am not a scrounger. I hate this situation. It seems to cut me off from my friends who have got jobs. I have to remind myself that God hasn't rejected me. He always has vacancies. Every one of us has infinite value to Him. There's always something worthwhile I can do in His Service. I must ask Him to help me, to help me now, today, to show me where to go and what to do next.

Prayer

Heavenly Father, Creator and Sustainer of everything, You made jobs for all Your sons and daughters to do, good, satisfying, worthwhile jobs, where we could help one another and get real satisfaction from doing it. Please help me to find one now. I ask it for Jesus' sake. Amen.

The Loneliness of Wealth

Our Lord Himself taught that it was easier for a camel to go through the eye of a needle — by which he probably meant the small gate in the city wall, suitable for pedestrians but almost impassable for a loaded camel — than it was for a rich man to enter the Kingdom of Heaven.

Riches are illusory and can be very deceptive.

To begin with what do we really mean by 'owning' something?

The little coral fish of the South Pacific reefs has a territorial imperative to defend his few square metres of underwater rock. He uses vast amounts of energy defending 'his' possessions. Yet the rocks were there long before he was hatched, and — unless Judgement Day comes before that — they will be there for thousands of years after the fish has died.

I may have millions in the bank, title deeds to thousands of acres of land, stocks and shares in everything from oil-wells to art galleries — yet what do I own in any real sense? Like the little coral fish, I'm only passing through: my overlordship of my possessions is as temporary as his. I may own a superb grand piano for which I paid £20,000, but can I play it?

Isn't the penniless young pianist who can play a Beethoven Sonata faultlessly more the master of my piano than I am? Do we 'own' things in any worthwhile sense unless we can understand them, and use them properly?

God is the only real owner of anything. He was here before the beginning. He is the Beginning. He will be here after the end. He is the End who has no ending. No one waits to inherit His possessions. He understands and makes perfect use of everything that He has made. He is the Master of all in every sense.

At the very best interpretation, all human ownership is only stewardship. God has given us charge of a few of His things for a short time. What we call wealth in human terms is only the degree of stewardship which we exercise under Him.

In many of our Lord's parables we are reminded that stewards are accountable. We are accountable. God will want to know one day what we have done with the property he gave us to look after for a while. Did the writer waste his talents producing cynical, bawdy blasphemy, or did he try to say something good and inspiring? Did the painter portray the mysterious beauty of the universe so well that you could almost see God behind his sunset, or did he set out to shock us with the ugly and the grotesque? Did the millionaire property developer set up housing schemes for the homeless, or pile up yet more office blocks for ever increasing profits? Did Dives share his good fortune with Lazarus, or leave him to die in the gutter with only the stray dogs for company? Dives had to answer for that. We shall all have to answer for what we have done with our earthly wealth.

Money can create impenetrable barriers between us and other people. We get to the point where we distrust them. Is he really my friend, or is he just after my money? Is he doing me a favour because he likes me, or because he wants something bigger in return?

Money can waste our lives for us in a meaningless rush of trivia which lie to us and tell us that they are vitally important. "Attend to me!" they scream from the pages of our diaries and appointment books. "I am an opportunity to sell, to charge a fee, to make money. You haven't time to stop and talk to people. Get on with business. Earn, work, sell, manufacture ... Make more money!" And when we've made it, what is it? Just another few metres of submarine coral to defend. Mammon is like the Wizard of Oz — nothing like as great as he wants people to think he is.

Christ warns us about money because He wants us to be happy. He wants us to enjoy His Fellowship and that of our brothers and sisters forever. He doesn't want us to waste our lives chasing illusions and cutting ourselves off from everything that brings true happiness. Take His advice. There is none better to be had anywhere. If we use our stewardship wisely, as God directs us, we can use our money to bring great joy to those less fortunate than ourselves, and in so doing find real happiness. Great material wealth can bring misery, isolation and loneliness with it unless we place our lives in Christ's keeping, and use our wealth in His service.

Poem and Prayer

I thank Thee Lord for blessing me
With this world's goods in store.
Teach me to use this wealth aright
And I shall thank Thee more.
Remind me of my stewardship,
However great my gain.
Remind me of the starving poor,
And of the sick man's pain.
Help me to share in Thy great work
Of generosity,
And then, Lord, on Thy Judgement Day,
Be generous to me,
Not for the sake of what I've done —
That merits no reward —
But for the sake of Jesus Christ,
My Saviour and my Lord.
Amen.

The Student Revising Alone

I seem to have dropped into some kind of limbo — or else this is a foretaste of purgatory. I daren't go out anywhere; I daren't watch television; I can't read a book I enjoy just for the pleasure of it — I must revise. The examination, that all-important, destiny-changing examination is so close now. I've worked so long and hard to get this far. I mustn't risk throwing it away now. I must exert every ounce of self-discipline I can muster. I have to pass this. Once it's over, I can relax and celebrate and have the time of my life, but until it's over I've got to work as if nothing else in the world existed. That's what make things so lonely.

I've had no social life for weeks. I'm turning into a bored and totally boring memorising machine. I just can't go on concentrating at this intensity forever. I've got to get this exam out of the way and have a real break. The horror of it is that I get too bored and tired to remember properly. I keep trying to make revision plans and revision time-tables, but the wretched syllabus is so wide, I simply can't cover it all. If I revised for ten years I don't think I could cover it all. I get desperate sometimes. I want to give it all up and become a taxi driver — but taxi drivers have to pass exams too! There's no escape any more: I'll just have to get down to it, I suppose, but, Lord, it's an awful job, and I'm so lonely shut away here with my books and my files of lecture notes.

Poem

I've read this page a dozen times, and still it makes no
    sense;
I wonder if I'm over-tired, or if I'm simply dense!
I've tried to use the formula in Figure Ninety-six:
But every answer's different and the constant's
    playing tricks.
I tried to use the other one, Example Sixty-four,
But when I differentiate I get a different score!
Now wasn't Januarius the god of doors and gates?
And there's something in November that Tiberius
    relates:
They tried to call it after him, and honour
    him by name —
But he asked what would happen if a thirteenth Caesar
    came!
I can't remember any more — it's dancing in my head.
I'll do some more tomorrow, but tonight I need my
    bed!

Prayer

Dear Lord of all lonely, tired and struggling people,
please help me. This revision is so important to me
—and to my family and friends as well. I have to pass
this exam, and I know that I can if I keep working at it,
but I am so tired, so bored and so lonely just now.
Grant me the strength to go on with it, dear Lord. You
showed us the way when You were on earth. You
never gave up. Grant me some of that strength and
determination that You had, Lord. Make me a true
soldier of Christ in my battle with this revision. I ask it
for His Sake. Amen.

Waiting Alone

Shakespeare was not the first thinker to notice how subjective time can be, but he certainly expressed the idea succinctly and elegantly: *"Time travels in divers paces with divers persons. I'll tell you who Time ambles withal, who Time trots withal, who Time gallops withal, and who he stands still withal."*

He stands still with the man or woman who waits alone. When we are waiting, the clocks freeze. The sand hangs motionless in the hour glass. The creeping shadow pauses on the sundial.

We may be waiting alone in an ecstasy of hope for some good news. We may be chilled at heart as we wait in dread for some bad news that we have feared for a long time. We may be waiting in an agony of suspense for news that could make us delirious with joy, or cast our spirits down to the lowest depths of despair.

We may be waiting for the results of important medical tests. We may be waiting for the results of an examination for which we have studied hard for a long time. We may be waiting for the selectors to decide whether to offer us a job or not, after years of unemployment. Even more important, we may be waiting to hear one of these answers not about ourselves but about someone we love so much that his or her life is infinitely more important to us than our own.

Waiting alone is incredibly hard to do. The longer we have to wait, the harder it gets. Remember the old Arabian story of the *djinn* in the sealed bottle who promised for the first thousand years of his imprisonment that he would make whoever freed him ruler of the world; for the second thousand years he mentally promised his rescuer endless youth and eternal life to go with his conquest of the world; but then he became embittered by the waiting — for the last thousand years he swore that whoever opened the bottle should be given no reward except that he would be allowed to choose how he wished to die — the punishment for keeping the *djinn* waiting so long!

Waiting can indeed be a desperate and embittering process — unless we are very careful to share the long, lonely, anxious hours with Christ. Our Lord knew what it was to wait: He waited in Gethsemane for Judas and the High Priest's guards. During that terrible time of waiting His sweat as He prayed became like great drops of blood. He Who knows better than any of us what a terrible experience waiting alone can be, is more than ready to share our waiting now. Ask Him. Invite Him. Just as we wait for news, or some major event, so He waits for us. God Himself is waiting for us, His little human creatures, to turn and look for Him, to speak to Him in prayer, to offer Him our worship. We know from Christ's own teaching that the repentance, the turning back to God, of just one sinner causes great rejoicing in Heaven. Incredible as it sounds, it is a simple statement of fact: the repentance of just one person is a major event in the Kingdom of Heaven.

How long should we who hate waiting ourselves expect our loving Heavenly Father to wait for us?

Poem

I have paced this floor like a caged tiger,
And the wild beast of my Impatience has clawed
At the locks and bars of unyielding circumstances
Until its frenzied nails broke in savage futility.
I have sat staring alone at a wall of such blankness
That even the eyes of my Impatience are blinded by it.
I will fight if I must, and suffer mortal wounding if I
     must,
But I can no longer wait and *do nothing*: I must *act* or die.
Christ waited alone in the Garden of Gethsemane,
Waited to die alone on a cross, at Golgotha,
Lay waiting alone in Joseph of Arimathea's tomb —
Then — all that *waiting* over at last — He arose
     triumphant.

Prayer

Lord Jesus Christ, suffering Saviour, You waited alone
so often and so long during Your earthly ministry.
Help me to wait when I have to. Be with me during the
worst of this waiting. Uphold me. Strengthen and
support me. Encourage and reinforce me. Reassure me
that whatever the outcome of this waiting, nothing
can separate me from You, and that at the end of all
waiting, I shall be with You and my loved ones forever,
and all shall be well. I ask it in Your Name. Amen.

Working Through the Night Alone

The closer we are to nature the happier we seem to be. It is as if there is a natural harmony between man and the created world God has given him. We experience rhythms, cycles and seasons and none perhaps more natural or more powerful than the constant rotation of day and night, of light and darkness. The human body responds to the changing pattern of night and day. The softly falling shadows beckon us to rest and sleep. The glory of the sunrise in the eastern sky awakens us to life and renewed activity.

However, we live in a technological society that has taken us away from the good old natural rhythms which we were built to follow. The unavoidable business of earning a living means that many of us have to work through the night: the journalist beating a deadline; the taxi driver at the big city station; the trucker dragging forty tons of freight up a midnight motorway; the nurse in the intensive care unit watching carefully and caringly as her patient struggles to maintain a vital flicker of life; the surgeon on night duty whose work she is supporting; the pilot with three hundred lives in his hands bringing his airliner safely down on to the runway at three a.m.; the milkman preparing for his round; the friar, the monk and the nun praying through the night; the policeman vigilant and protective; the electrical engineer struggling to restore torn cables; and the sailor on his night watch battling through the Bay of Biscay in a force nine.

It feels strange to work while others sleep; to go to one's labours not in the brightness of the sun but by the pale light of the moon, the stars and the street lamps. So many of the tasks that we undertake at night are of vital importance for the wellbeing of society. Those of us who work while others sleep, who face the loneliness that comes from working what are sometimes called 'unsociable' hours, have this reassurance: the labours of the night are the seeds from which the life of the following day grows. Those who toil by night are separated from their brothers and sisters who work in the normal daylight hours only by the hands of the clock and the rising and setting of the sun: workers of the night and workers of the day are united by their dependence upon one another. The worker who toils in the dark is in some ways like the lonely ploughman who prepares the field for the sower; the workers of the day are the harvestmen working in groups together, aware of one another's fellowship and shared activity. Yet without the lonely ploughman and the sower there could be no harvest. It is often harder to work alone while others sleep, than to share our toil with a group of friends and colleagues. Yet the lonely work of the night must go on.

God Himself never sleeps; His love for us is constant and unending. The Angels and Ministers of Grace are ever attentive to their Lord's command. The day and the night are both alike to Him.

Poem

I work through the darkness, while other men sleep;
My guard and my vigil I faithfully keep.
A hand on the tiller, head on to the storm,
I battle the oceans while landsmen lie warm.
The rhythm and cycle of daytime and dark —
Work makes me an owl, though my nature is lark.
I pull forty tons up a dark mid-night road:
Tomorrow the shoppers will purchase my load.
My hand holds the scalpel that saves and restores;
The nurse holds the needle, the thread and the gauze.
His mother gives thanks in the pale morning light
For the accident victim I saved in the night.

Prayer

Lord, help me to remember as I toil alone through this
long weary night that You are with me. Lord, as I keep
my vigil through the darkness, help me to remember
that as I watch over others so You are watching over
me. Make me ever more aware of Your presence with
me, loving Lord. Show me that with You beside me, I
have nothing to fear in the darkness or the light. Help
me to remember that although I cannot often see my
brothers and sisters who work by day, our work unites
us and we are one in You. I ask it for the sake of Jesus
Christ my Lord. Amen.

Writing Alone – The Lure of the Diary

At some time or another we all have the irresistible urge to be Samuel Pepys or Parson Woodford: we decide to become a diarist. If we have the singular gifts of Woodford and Pepys to go with the urge, then what we write will be of vast interest and value to posterity. My old friend and mentor, that extremely talented Norwich writer, Harry Mansfield, (who is now with the Lord) was approached by some elderly friends of his a few years ago because they had found an ancient diary in a shed at their home. When Harry investigated, it turned out to be the actual manuscript diary of an officer who had served in the Crimean War. With great skill and patience Harry deciphered it, annotated it and ultimately published it: a unique primary source for historians specialising in the period. What drove that Crimean War soldier to write as he did, so long ago and so far from his Norfolk home? The same urge that takes us all from time to time — the lure of the diary.

There are, of course, dozens of reasons for keeping a diary. It is good, worthwhile and interesting to record what we have done. It can be very useful to refer to it again for scores of reasons. In George Orwell's "1984" it was a serious offence for a citizen in that terrible totalitarian state to keep a diary. If citizens kept diaries, they might start to argue with the state propaganda machine when it told them that something hadn't happened when it had!

It is very pleasant at family get-togethers for the diary keeper to announce something like, "It was exactly five years ago today that we all went to Sally's Wedding together." My mother is a great diary keeper; and my late sister Mona used to be.

Keeping a diary is an intimation of immortality. The urge that we have to write things down is no accident. Our desire to keep a record is a reflection of that instinctive, God-given feeling we have that records are worth keeping because life is worth living. Human beings are not disposable. Life has a meaning. Individual lives have meanings. We desire to record things because things are important — even the tiniest details have significance, especially to God. "The very hairs of your head are all numbered," says our Lord. He teaches us that God cares even for the sparrows and the lilies of the field: so he certainly cares for us. The Incarnation and Christ's work of salvation at Calvary show us most clearly of all how much God cares about us. If we are as important as that to Him, the events which fill up our lives are important enough to fill up the pages of our diaries.

When we are alone, making an entry on a diary page, let us think of it in this way: God our Father loves and cares for us more than we can even begin to imagine. We are loved with an Everlasting Love. His interest in us is total.

His commitment to our salvation is total. Every detail of our lives is of major significance to Him. We do not need to say anything in our prayers, because He knows what we want and need even before we ask. We do not need to show Him our diaries because He knows everything that we have done, said and thought. Yet He loves to hear our prayers, and He loves to share the events of our days with us. Think of a page in your diary as your daily report to Him — share it with God, just as you share the memories of interesting anniversaries with your earthly friends and family. The water of everyday life changes to wine when it comes into contact with God.

Prayer

Most loving and caring God, our Heavenly Father, here in my diary I have recorded the events of the day, as they seemed to me, and as I understood them. Pardon all that I have done wrong this day. Forgive my sins, remembered and forgotten. Forgive any thoughtless act which has grieved Your Loving Heart, or hurt my brothers and sisters in any way. I offer You this diary as an imperfect and incomplete symbol of my imperfect and incomplete life. Help me to fill my days better. Inspire my mind with higher thoughts, my heart with nobler feelings, and my soul with deeper and more urgent longing for You. Lord may these records of my fleeting earthly days help me to learn from my mistakes and so prepare me for the perfect, endless days of Heaven, for the sake of Christ, my Lord. Amen.

Unable to Sleep

Sleep is one of God's greatest and most precious gifts.

Poets have written some of their finest lines in its praise. When all else fails to correct the stresses and strains of the working day, sleep is our superbly effective physician.

But that superbly effective physician and his assistants, Sister Comfort and Nurse Quietness, are not always on call when we need them most. That very physical or mental exhaustion for which sleep is the best remedy may itself be driving away any chance of repose.

The torment of our loneliness when we are unable to sleep only aggravates and increases our insomnia. In that useless, barren darkness of the empty bedroom a thousand worries wash over our minds on the fretful waves of self-pity. We regret the past. We fear the future. We resent the present. We doubt God and we doubt ourselves. Faith is weak and temptation is strong. Life never seems more pointless and unfair than it does to the lonely sleepless mind. We are at our most vulnerable to Satan's cunning innuendos and gloomy, Godless misrepresentations of the real state of affairs in the universe.

What can we actually do about it next time it happens?

First we can use the time profitably. Send your thoughts where you want them to go instead of letting them wander painfully among mental weeds, nettles and briars. They're your thoughts after all. You're the boss. The will controls the mind, not vice versa. That's what being a real man or woman is all about. You choose. You make it happen. Point your thoughts to beauty, truth and love — and to your God Who is the Creator and Sustainer of all beauty, truth and love.

Second, we can direct our thoughts and emotions away from the succulent trough of selfishness towards which we instinctively gravitate whenever we feel sorry for ourselves instead of feeling sorry for others. Think of others. Do it deliberately. Do it now. Get your thoughts away from your own wants and needs. Look outside yourself. Think positively about whether there is anything at all you can do to help someone you know. You may not be able to do very much, but the smallest of things can be of immense value — especially to someone else who is feeling as lonely and as miserable as you are. It is infinitely better to get out of bed and begin a long overdue letter of encouragement to a friend in hospital a long way away than to lie in oppressive darkness and nurture your misery.

Loneliness and misery are very responsive patients: the more attention they get, the more vigorously they thrive. Turn your back on them and they begin to shrink and pine away from sheer neglect.

Third, we can try all the sensible old-fashioned remedies for insomnia, the ones our parents and grandparents taught us: a glass of hot milk with malt in it; a good, relaxing book like Jerome K. Jerome's "Three Men in a Boat" or the Grossmiths' "Diary of a Nobody"; a warm, leisurely bath — or even a combination of all three. There is all the difference in the world between pampering ourselves with a few well-deserved little luxuries like these (which God has put here for our enjoyment in any case) and indulging ourselves in an orgy of melancholy, misery and self-pity. Our self-hood, like everything else God has made for us, is intended to enable us to experience those vast pleasures which His love wants us to enjoy: deliberately wallowing in misery and self-pity during our sleepless loneliness is as much a misuse and abuse of the self as the emission of nuclear radiation and fluorocarbons is a misuse and abuse of the planet.

Prayer

O ever vigilant and wakeful Lord, Thy servant cannot rest, cannot receive Thy gift of sleep. Please grant me that peace which the world cannot give so that I may relax completely. Show me that the darkness and the light are both alike to Thee. Turn my thoughts to love and truth and beauty, and most of all towards Thee, from Whom all good things come. So fill me with Thy love and peace that all cares and worries are driven from me. Remind me that with Thee and companies of blessed Saints and Angels I can never be truly alone. Amen.